So Many Things to Say

A Collection of Poems

by

LeJuane Bowens

authorHOUSE®

AuthorHouse™
1663 Liberty Drive, Suite 200
Bloomington, IN 47403
www.authorhouse.com
Phone: 1-800-839-8640

First published by AuthorHouse 6/27/2007

ISBN: 978-1-4343-1487-1 (sc)

Printed in the United States of America
Bloomington, Indiana

This book is printed on acid-free paper.

Dedication:

It's hard to begin where to start off. Everything has had an inspiration to me in helping me put this together. But, if I were to break down the important things and people that have inspired me in my life, it would be these people. To God, for being the force that drove me into seeing the gifts that was bestowed upon me through him. I thank you. To my mother and father for bringing me into this world and loving me for what they've created. To Grandma Elnora, you made me the man that I've grown to be. There should be a word that expresses gratitude more than love. To Isaiah and Jalen, my two handsome sons. Daddy is always trying to make you two proud of him so this should just be another notch on the belt. I love you two. To Crystal. Baby, you are the reason that I found love again and without the love you've giving me, I would be a heartless bastard. My friendship will always belong to you. To Dr.Olien, you blessed me with a better understanding of rhyme, song, and soul. I wish this were an album but maybe in time that will come. Thank you. My Shorty, you and you alone know what joy you brought into my life in a place where it was joyless to begin. Thank you for you being there when I needed you most and I hope it'll be like that for years to come. And last, but not least, to all my friends, associates, and especially the ex's. One saying that I love to go by is this; Hardship is what made me, but it's your love that keeps me going. You are the ones that painted the canvas of my soul and what made me write again. Isn't that something? Well, that's about it. If I left anyone out, I'll make sure to get at you next time(if there's demand that there will be a next time for me) or just add your name here_____.Hope that all of you readers enjoy what you read. Now, without further a due, on with the show.

Contents

So Many Things to Say... iii

Dedication: v

Why I Write..1

Words of A Poet 2

Addiction 3

1st Decision..4

Overcome 5

A Good Parent 6

What's The Point...7

D.D. 8

Change..9

Emotion..10

Whole 11

One-Way Discussion 12

My Plea: A Message To God 13

One Nation Under 14

My Favorite Song...15

Love, Life, and Happiness 17

On The Outside Looking In...18

Teardrops 19

Soldier...21

Shut Down...22

Escape From Within 23

For What It's Worth 24

Mask 25

Remember..26

Prison..28

A Rose...29

This Thing Called Love 30

Don't Ever Change 31

To Want A Friend 32

My Meaning 33

My Shorty..35

Love on a Jagged Edge..37

The Long Kiss Good Night 38
Let's Just Say..39
What I See..... 41
As One..42
Her Trance 43
Behind Closed Doors 45
Love Session 47
Pleasurable 49
The Perfect Storm..50
Morning Bliss...51
In Control..52
Craving 54
Negative & Plus 55
S.T.D 56
A Hidden Agenda 57
I Must Not Be There 58
Forget Everything..59
It Is What It Is. 60
By Myself...61
The Other One 62
Phone Check...63
What Did I Do? 65
Consequence 66
Hard To Let Go..68
Prison...69
Five Minutes 70
Space...72
What Will It Take.... 74
It (A Woman's Story) 75
Beginnings 77

Why I Write

I write because it's my release,
My release from all of the constant pain,joy,love,hardship,
And tension that builds up from the unsettling base
Of B.S. that surrounds me on a day to day basis.
I write because it let's you know that beneath the exterior
You see, beats the heart of a normal man.
A man with everyday problems
Everyday struggles
But through it all, I always find
Everyday solutions.
I write because it's a natural high that I don't ever want to
Come down from.
It puts me at ease and makes my heart feel pure and full of
Happiness and warmth
Like the embrace from the one you love
Or warm taste of Grandma's apple pie after it comes
From the oven.
I write because of what you, the people feel
Because without a voice, theses feelings will never become
Substance,flesh,real
And it order for that to happen, it needs to be heard and felt
Through the eyes of the reader who reads these thoughts
Put to life on paper.
I write because it's my release.
And now that it's released,
I hope that it overflows into the world
And that everyone can accept
In abundance, what is about to overcome them.
And that my friend........is freedom through words.
This is what I am
And this is why I write

Words of A Poet

You think you know,
But you have no idea,
No, this isn't an MTV:Dairy episode,
But this is more of an explanation,
You read what you read as if,
You are actually looking through my own eyes,
When in actuality, this is just like music,
Just like movies, just like entertainment in it's own.
I'll admit, sometimes what I write may deal with a life experience,
And at times, it's just a figment of the imagination,
But what you fail to understand is that I write because I want to be
heard,
I write because I give to you what most people would go through,
Maybe me, maybe you.
For you may not have the voice to say what you want to say,
You got to realize, poets are all not people who
Write what they write because we feel you need to
Get into their life.
Because if you really look at it,
we're just storytellers on another level.
So don't get the misconception that what you're reading now is a true
statement.
But then again, what if it is?
I'll let you be the judge of that.

Addiction

I dream about it night and day
A craving in my life that I don't want to go away

Coursing through my veins every time it hits me
It's like an old Negro spiritual made to uplift me

Infatuated with this addiction from within
That it seeps through my pores and sits upon my skin

I twitch when I can't have it then and there
It makes me begin to stress me out and pull out my hair

My palms are wet and my face turns pale
Not being around it seems like its pure hell

No ward or asylum can cure this affliction
It makes me whole. It's like simple addition

My lips done got to the point that they've turned powder white
The sight of it sparks my interest that it leaves my mind burning bright

So, what's this addiction that rest deep within
It's the addiction to write. The addiction to bring you in

My mind, my heart, my soul. Put on blast
Now, my addiction is your addiction. How long do you want it to last?

1st Decision.........

So, another day, same old life,
Not much of it has changed,
Or has it?
Think about it,
You grow up through K-12
Doing things that you were raised to do.
But what happens when you're out on your own,
When You got to make That 1st decision
A decision that judges then and there
The person you may become.
Whether it's something simple like
Buying groceries or crossing the street
Or more complex like who to give love to or
Whether or not to quit your job.
It sounds as simple as day to think about
The complexities of what one person
One soul, one body could accomplish in a day
A week, A year, A Decade
A century. But when it's all said and done
When the time runs out on life and you reflect on what you may Or
may not have accomplished in
life.
It always come back
I repeat,
It always comes back.
To that 1st decision

Overcome

We all have our faults,
But through all of our problems,
We find our way through.

A Good Parent

What do you think
Labels you a good parent?
Is it because you call every now and then?
Is it because you pay child support when it's due?
Is it because you tell every body when you get around them
That you have a child and that you love him so much?
Those are just physical things that you do
To cover up the truth of the matter at hand.
It's not about just doing these things that makes you a parent.
You have to physically & emotionally be there when we need you
most.
You can call every now and again
But what good is a call when you can visit on your free time when
you have it?
What's good about paying child support
When you can just make sure we have what we need without a court
ordering you to do so.
What good is telling your friends about the child you love so much
When in turn, you don't let your friends ever see us besides the
picture you show them.
If you really love me as a parent then prove it.
Love me for more than just being your seed.
Love me for being the very essence of life itself
Love me for being the future of our family and becoming something
great
Love me for me being a child of God and that when the time comes,
I'll be in the same shoes you are in and tell the next generation to
come
That I love them for who they are and what I want them to be.........
Successful and proud.
By you doing those things for me, that will label you in my eyes,
As a good parent

What's The Point

What's the point of having things that have no meaning?
What's the point of loving someone when they don't love you back?
What's the point of world peace when we can't have peace amongst
each other?
What's the point of turning the other cheek knowing that a person
can't let a grudge go away easy?
What's the point of making promises when they are always empty?
What's the point of telling someone you want more, just to only get
so little?
What's the point of me writing this poem and you may never read
this?
What's the point of having friends when they are really associates?
Honestly, what's the point?

D.D.

The game's what made me,
Loving how I make money,
Hustling cocaine

Change

I've always heard the saying,
That a change is going to come,
But at what price will it,
The price of someone's soul perhaps,
Who knows what to say?
Change is the means of knowing that everything,
Including life, is not always meant,
To stay on the same path,
To know that everything is destined to be different,
The essence of time continuously spinning,
Going through the same rotation
Spinning on its same axis,
And yet, we evolve. Timid and scared
Because the life that we live is not scripted, not planned.
But like before, destined to change
Watching old friends grow old as you grow old
Becoming a parent and understand the meaning of sacrificing
Time because now, you have a bigger responsibility than your own
Losing all of the old bad habits and picking up new ones
To make you a better you..
These are the things to expect, endure, and embrace.
So the question is……..
Are you ready for a change?

Emotion

People,

I've been in a funk lately.

Letting little b.s. get into what is important to me.

But that's what happens when you deal with a lot of people that you try to make feel.

I don't need to get into details because some things do not need to be explained.

But you know how I act, and you know what I can do when it comes down to it.

I'll make you smile when I need to, or I can make you cry when the time is right for it to happen.

Makes you think doesn't it? What the hell am I'm talking about? Where am I coming from?

I'm just stating the obvious. I live a hard life wondering how it feels to feel what you feel.

Now I know you're confused, but hear me out;

For once I would like to know what's it like to be angry, to be in love, to be scared,

And to feel Joy wherever I wanted.

So for people, I envy you for having something only I can give you

But cannot have myself in my own existence; and that is what I am.

Emotion

Whole

Make me whole,
Make me more of a man than what I once was,
Make me understand that with time and patience,
I will be more than just a vessel
More than just a figure of flesh,blood,sweat,and tears.
Make me make sense of this life that I've been destined to see
through my eyes as I view them. Make me accomplish more than just
a
Simple task that can easily be done away with like throwing away
garbage
Or simply just waking up in the morning.
I can't even say that because that is an accomplishment that's not easy
Because nothing is always guaranteed.
And that's why I want to become a whole man
Because pieces of me have been chipped away at like clay.
But, now that I think about it, there's nothing wrong with that.
Because I need to chip away what's bad in my life
So that it may make me the work of art that I want to become.
And that is to become whole.

One-Way Discussion

Who am I to choose?
Who am I to be the one to dictate what you should do with your life?
You are a grown person who can make there own decision in life.
I can't be the one to decide that for you.
As much as I try to influence you to do the right thing
Who am I to choose?
Who am I to be the one to dictate what you should do with your life?
You are a grown person who can make there own decision in life.
I can't be the one to decide that for you.
As much as I try to influence you to do the right thing
You are the one who can really decide that factor.
I try my best to give you signs of what's to come
Without really coming out and giving you an answer
Because I will be taking you away from what may be destined to you
And that couldn't find it in me to do such a thing
Especially since you have free will and that's one thing that I'll never
do
And that is force it upon you because I want you to make decisions
on your own.
But still, I hope in my heart that you do the right thing when you can
Heh, this is fumy to me because this is the first time I've talked to
Anyone like how I'm talking right now.
I guess this is the only way that I can come across to you.
But let's just end this conversation. I have to let you be who you are
Just know that I will be watching over you to make sure you're ok.
And hopefully, before it gets too late
You will find in your heart where you need to be.
Bless you my child.

God.

My Plea: A Message To God

I love you so much my Lord,
And I don't want You to think that I'm drifting away,
It's just that the flesh of temptation in this world I live on,
Is implanting thoughts that could lead me astray.

I love you so much Lord,
I want all of Your glorious love in my heart,
And to know that I'm loved by a graceful force of life itself,
Let's me know that our bond will not be torn apart.

I love you more than anything physical,
Cause without you, my life is nothing,
And for you to forgive and rain down Your precious love,
Makes me feel like I'm worth something.

I love you and there's no doubt about it,
That's why I come to you with this plea,
To state that through the darkness that presents itself,
You will always find a light in me.

I'll never lose my faith in You,
And I pray that you don't lose your faith in me,
To keep me and all men in your heart,
And love every one of us for all eternity.

I love you counting five to six times over,
And still, that will not be enough for just one man,
But know that my heart is pure and you are why I live,
In your name, we pray. Amen

One Nation Under

We find these truths
To be self-evident
Well, if that is the case
Tell me where the government money is spent

Tell me why we have a national debt,
But yet, we still have money to spend
Why do we have people in this nation
That's not even willing to lend

Something to their fellow man when he's down and out
And trying to get his/her life together
Why can't this nation look past its selfishness
And try to make life for us all better

Why do we continue to fight a war
When we are fighting a war within ourselves
Not realizing that we're writing two wrongs
Not realizing that within our hearts, this concept dwells

Then, we say that we're a nation under God
But, God does not hate on a different race,creed,or religion
There's still racism under this nation that we live in
And it still affects us like a head-on collision

So, keep all these in mind,
And try not to forget this while you slumber
Because when it seems like we may be a nation under God
It feels like we're just one nation under..............

My Favorite Song...

My favorite song consist of a melody

That everyone would love to hear

A melody of peace and happiness

That makes people hold what they cherish dear

A song that would actually mean

Much more to life than just words

Much more than just material things

Much more than everything that's already been heard

It brings the best out of you

When you feel pain in your heart

And opens up your mind and soul

To separate the good and bad apart

Every note would be in harmony

And every word you will be able to feel

As if it materialized itself into something

That you would be able to hold and feel.

It would bring tears to your eyes

Regardless if you're bitter and hard

And mend the physical and emotional wounds

That you may feel were left permanently scared.

Never skipping a beat or rhythm

And something that can be played always regardless how long

This is what that means to me..........

This is my favorite song

Love, Life, and Happiness

Love without a plan,
Life without known boundaries,
Happiness remains.

On The Outside Looking In

How can you sit there judge
Making assumptions of someone and then hold a grudge

Beginning to gain hatred for something you don't understand
So you take it out upon your fellow man.

Bottling it inside yourself to the point that you can't keep it within
All because of you being on the outside looking in.

Looking at a concept that holds to be false
Letting your ego get the best of you and at the end, it's going to cost

Friendships with friends because you're hating there accomplishments
Because you don't have what they have. This leaves you in astonishment

But in actuality, it's all on you
Because you didn't get off of your ass to do what you needed to do

Thinking that in life that you could get around
With only your charm and other's hand me downs

Take an initiative and get up and get out
Do something with YOUR life instead of staying on this negative route

Blaming others for your own faults and mistakes
When just getting your life in order is all that it takes

So look at yourself in the mirror and look deep within'
And get yourself out from the outside looking in.

Teardrops

Streaming down the side of my face.
When I comprehend that day.
That day that plays in my mind like any other.
A day that bring sadness to not only me,
But those around who also feel the affects.
I feel at times God feels what I feel
Because it is at that moment when gray clouds form
And the rain begins to come down all over
Making life seem emptier and shell less
An empty vessel within itself
More and more it burns inside
To know that you're not here anymore
And I could think of the all the things I wish
I could have done different.
Take back certain decisions that I made
Or turn back time for just a few seconds may have prevented This
outcome of uncertainty.
I'm wishing that I could tell you that I love you
Just one more time.
Hold you in my arms for just a while longer
To show you that your affection means the world
To me and I could never ask for nothing more
Than for your love.
But sometimes life isn't planned out the way we
Want it to be.
And I just want you to know that life goes on
And I will be okay and I want you
To push on, but not forget about me
Because I will never forget you
And the love that you put inside my heart
And brought into my life.
But you will know when I'm sad
Because when you see the sky turn gray,

Just run outside, look up at the sky,
And close your eyes and think of me
Because this isn't just rain,
These are my teardrops.
And you being there to catch them let me know
That there's still love there
And that one day, we will be together
And this will bring the sunshine back into my life.

Soldier

I feel as if I was put on this earth,
To defend and uphold what is true,
And now that I am realizing this vision,
I know the decision I had made was the right thing to do.

Cause now I'm standing in a position,
With bullets flying over my head,
Mortars exploding and IED's all around,
Ready to claim someone for dead.

But regardless of the wartime struggles,
And the choices that determines right from wrong,
I retain the courage to stand tall as a soldier,
I remain to stand strong.

Continuously promising all of my loved ones,
That I will be back to see them,
And the reason that I am over here fighting,
Is to insure them of their freedom.

I swear that I will be on my way back home,
Once peace and freedom here is won,
Against all enemies, foreign and domestic,
This is the pledge that I swore to get done.

So when the odds got me against the wall,
And the weight of the world seem to sit on my shoulders,
I will remain to stay vigilant,
I will stand strong as a soldier.

Shut Down

I was never the one to be called cute,
Let alone, being handsome was never something absolute,

No woman on Earth would pay me no mind,
Or even attempt to give me the time

No group of friends would allow me by there side,
Or if they seen me coming, they would run and hide

Afraid of me bringing their popularity down,
I guess that's why they didn't want me around.

A modern day ugly duckling I was to become,
Because everyone made me out to be just ugly and dumb.

Not realizing the change that was soon to happen,
That would have everyone stop all their laughing.

For I'm a better man than what I used to be
Strong and handsome for all of the world can see.

All of these people that had played me for a fool
Are now in my face as if we were once cool.

Every female that would have never gave me a chance at all,
Are throwing numbers at my feet.Saying,"Baby, give me a call".

Speaking gibberish about how they've missed me being at home
When in actuality, they never even knew that I was gone.

Until they saw me on television
That is what made these hypocrites come to their decision.

To come in my face. But now, you're the one's whose getting clowned
Cause now I'm doing to y'all what y'all done to me. I'm shutting you down

Escape From Within

Racing to my destination
Beating out all those who stand in my way
Overcoming the obstacles of this long journey
To attempt to cement in this world a mark stating that I'm here to stay

Reaching my goal within due time
Only to realize that this was just a trap
A plot put together so maliciously
And now,there's no turning back

I heard of something like this from the voices I hear
Being contained with no escape
A prison or something of that nature
Where all you can do is contemplate

Now I have to find a way out
So I can once again be free
I must think of a way to escape
This space in which contains me

Days,weeks,and months go by
And this space I'm in is beginning to close in
And with all the constant change that has happened within that time
I feel my time will eventually come to an end.

But to my surprise,a light has appeared
And I find myself sliding out with joy.
But then,a man in white slaps me and I begin to cry
And he hands me to a lady and says,"It's a boy"

For What It's Worth

For What It's Worth,
I guess that I can tell you now,
That this goes beyond the physical,
But more on the emotional,
My soul at this moment is battered to a pulp,
By the constant changes that bring dark clouds
Into what was once a beautiful life.
I can't even begin to fathom the fact
That once again, I'm alone in this world,
Same old story, only a new damn year,
But in the end that what It boils to right,
Regardless of how much time you put in,
Or how much effort you give,
You are destined to get almost nothing for it.
And you ask me,
Why do I always have a picture by myself looking so sad,
Its because of a known truth in my life,
That no matter What I do, say, or accomplish,
I'll always be on my own.
For what it's worth

Mask

Why hide your own face,
Don't play false to impress folks,
Wear your own true mask.

Remember

Take this time to reflect
About the things that you did
In life, in general
Since you were a kid

Remember the times you had
When you were happy and sad
Remember the love that you get
From your mom and your dad

Remember when gas was about
A dollar and change
And the things around you
That you were hoping to stay the same.

Remember a summer back when
When your family got together,
Grilling up at the park
And you were down to do whatever

Remember when you were about to
Commit to love
And your friends would laugh at you
Treating you like a scrub

When in actuality,
They were really only jealous
Cause you spend some time with him or her
Instead of with the girls or fellas.

Remember going through school
And everything was fine
Till you hit your senior year
And seeing your friends for the last time.

This is just a little taste
Of what your mind can dismember
So do yourself some justice
And take this time to just remember.

Prison

Never seeing light,
Four walls closing in so close,
Trapped inside my cell

A Rose

Starting off as the sapling seed
You try to establish what you will need

In order to make you bloom to perfection
And above else, surpass all expectation

For those who may seem to see
You for youth and childhood glee

When what they fail to understand
Is that this is not part of the plan.

The plan for you is to outgrow adolescence
Establish a base of beauty and evanescence

But as you begin to grow, the thorns of life,
Grow along with you and bring within what's trife.

Hardship,pain,sadness,despair
All in which we as people have to bare,

But not you cause through it all
All of these will not make you fall.

And the happiness returns to shine,
Blinding all the troubles and bringing to you in time,

Elegance,exquisiteness,radiance,and care
An abundant source of love that will always be there.

Now the time is now and your time is here
Where you venture into the world my dear

Behold a lady, in which this world has chose
A tiny seedling that has now become a rose.

This Thing Called Love

This is weird, you know.
Kind of a hard feeling to express
This thing called Love
I guess it's what I'm feeling at this moment.
Cause of the things I do I guess.
I mean, I do think about you constantly,
You are the 1st thing that pops up in my mind every morning
I do cherish every millisecond that I'm with you too.
The nights at the movies, the long walks in the park,
The 12 hour conversations of what we can see ourselves doing
In the long run.
Wow....................
This really is love. I mean, I hope it is
I don't want this to be some sort of long dream that I have to wake up
from.
I don't want this to be like a freak accident that going to leave my
body
Numb to the bone and at the same time, paralyzing my heart.
I just want you to meet me halfway on this self-discovery
And not let me be the one to take this trip alone.
Take my hand and let's take this journey together.
I'm not asking you to marry me or nothing.
I just want you to be where I am.
And embrace this thing that over joys our hearts,
This thing called Love.

Don't Ever Change

We have been through so much. I swear we have,
But now, when I look into your eyes,
All I see is a beautiful sun
Setting in the sky.

And with your personality and astounding beauty,
I hope that you will never change,
As we begin to grow older,
And take our love through the next stage.

Because as time change, we begin to change,
But our love will always remain the same,
No matter how painful life's hurdles are thrown on our path,
We will overcome the pain.

To complete this lifetime as one,
Two single lives living together,
Being as one, working in harmony,
Continuously growing stronger. Forever

So, I'm asking you, don't change up on me,
And my love for you will always be there,
I fell for who you are and not for what you do,
So don't worry about me going anywhere.

We live in order to feel,
And I feel your love coursing through my veins,
We've come together to grow old together,
And that's why this love won't ever change.

To Want A Friend

I'm doing all I can to fight,
This feeling that I'm feeling for you,
Too conscious and scared to speak on it,
Because I'm afraid that it not be true.

We've been around one another as close friends,
And it has made me want you more,
If this feeling was based on fishing,
I would be drawn to your lore.

Cause of all the fishes in the sea as they say,
I'm the one that has caught on,
Never wanting to let this go,
Cause both of our holds is so strong.

And just when it seems I'm about to pull away,
You begin to reel me back in,
No matter how much I begin to tug away,
You grasp me from with your strength from within.

So maybe we can try to begin life a new,
And treat this like a new beginning,
A life that will have no boundaries,
Like book which doesn't have an ending.

Cherishing the feelings we have,
And attempt to make it last till the end,
And regardless of us being a couple,
You will first, and always, be my friend.

My Meaning

I found a meaning now,
And I found it in you,
Anxiously awaiting in life,
For this moment to come true,

I used to question God at times,
If you were sent from above,
Because you have brought me so much happiness,
But yet I haven't said to you what it is I love,

I love how we fuss and fight,
But only for play and not for real,
I love how I can tell you any and everything
Cause you can relate to any ordeal

I love how you let me hold you
When we lay together ay night,
Promising you that I will be by your side
As I begin to embrace your body tight

I love it that you speak your mind
And that you don't need to hold your tongue,
I love how independent you are
To the point that you need nothing from no one

But I love it when you say you love me
Cause I hope that your love does exist
It's been a while since I been around true love
And tasted upon true love's kiss

And nothing taste more sweeter,
Than your lips against mine,
Leaving a hint of Brown Sugar

That sends a tingle down my spine.

So that's what your love mean to me
And I hope it stays this way
I love you with all of my heart
And I hope this feeling doesn't go away

My Shorty

My Shorty.
An unimaginable phenomenal woman she is.
The last fraction in my life which has completed me
And has made me a whole being.
I never have to worry about the stresses of work
Because when I see her, she makes all the troubles of the world
Seem to not even exist to me anymore.
She takes me to a place where everything is perfect
And there is not a dark cloud in the sky.
She holds me in her arms when she sees that I've had
A hard day or just to show me that she's happy to see me
Come home to her everyday in one piece.
She kisses me to let me know that there is always passion
Resting behind those lips of an angel that's only meant for
Me and me alone and that no one is deserving of her love but me.
She looks me into my eyes and I look back into hers.
At this time, our souls our insuring themselves of the future in which
we
Plan to make with each other and not let anything get in the way in
what
We feel is rightfully ours, and that is the love that we planted in our
Hearts and watch grow since we both instilled this seed within us.
I never need to worry about if she would leave me
Or me leaving her
Because we've been through too much in life together.
The arguments in the beginning, the pressure of friends
Thinking that we're moving fast in the relationship,
The men and women that would see us together
And try to do their best to try and come between us
Because they don't want to see us happy and
Rather than us being together, they would rather see us apart
So that they can come in and capitalize on the love we started for you
& me.
Most would consider you to be the wifey type because of what I wrote

But a wifey is not what I'm looking for.
Because I would rather have something solid in my heart
Than something that can easily get taken away from me
Through a disagreement and a court order.
So this is what I have, regardless of what paper may say
Or what some document may have annotated.
You are what I've always wanted. A woman to be there to the end.
Not my wifey, but my shorty

Love on a Jagged Edge

I used to think to myself
What's it like to be in love
Always thinking that I gotta be the one
Wanting to be the one whose love was so hard
But at times I found myself trying to find the words
Because it was hard to explain to you face to face
I used to have visions of the good and bad
Knowing that nothing is promised to me & you
I don't wanna live without and love nobody else
That's why you always get a remedy from me
A remedy that gives you that special healing you need
So what you trying to do with me baby
What choice do you wanna make for us
If you were to leave it would feel like I've just
Walked right outta heaven
But in the end, it's all a dream to me
Because in the morning when we wake up
You'll be looking at me so peacefully
This is where we need to be
Baby, you are so amazing to me
And in time, I'll say to you
Let's get married and then and only then
Will you realize that you are everything I've asked for In this life of
bad luck.
You're my good luck charm
This is why I wrote this to you.
Because I couldn't say this from my own words
So I took these words from a group you love
And presented this poem to you.
Don't believe me
Reread it and think about it.

The Long Kiss Good Night

It's the last thing that I can remember giving,
The last thought and action I can recall,
And cherish till I leave this Earth,
But before it happened, I remember how it started,
As a heated argument over nothing,
I was just being a man about things and figured,
Everything must go my way,
Not realizing the fact before this happened,
This contemplation of things to be and things that are not,
Every relationship has ups and downs,
And some work out for the best,
But that shouldn't drive me to do things on impulse like
Drink, make love to someone else, or kill someone,
Lord knows I haven't and I don't plan on it,
I now know that I messed up for screaming at you,
And I apologize for that, And that is why I give you this
As a reminder of what could have been and why I'm glad that it's not,
Our love that has stayed through it all,
And that is why I held you till the next day and will
Always remember when an argument almost turned into,
The Long Kiss Good Night

Let's Just Say

Let's just say that we started talking,

Would that make you think different of me,

Let's just say that we made love one night together,

Would it be everything that you wanted it to be.

Let's just say that I brought you around my friends,

Would you smile because I stayed true,

Would it make you happy that I didn't put on a front,

To impress them instead of caring for you.

Let's just say that we were out in public,

Would you cry if I got down on one knee,

And took a ring from out of my pocket,

And tell you that forever, I want you to be here with me.

Let's just say that we had a child,

Whether it be a girl or a boy,

Would you feel blessed to see that we're a perfect family,

Wouldn't that be the greatest feeling in the world.

But let's just say that we talked about all this,

And that our friendship wasn't in the way,

And that we really felt this way for each other,

But for now, let's just say.

What I See.....

What I see is a vision of something so pure,

That its cleanses my heart and makes me endure,

The love and affection that you bring into my life,

Which seems like a rumor, cause I'll believe the hype.

You make me feel so young inside,

And you bring me joy, which my face cannot hide,

Why hide these feelings on feeling complete,

When it's your love that knocks me on my feet.

I feel more alive when I see you smile,

And if you moved far away, I would walk that long mile,

To see the radiance that glows from you.

You must be a dream because this cannot be true.

But it is very real, and I'm Glad that it is,

Cause this is a feeling I cannot resist,

Because of you, you have completed me,

And when I look into your eyes, This is all of what I see.

As One

Kissing you gently,
Fierce, passionate love making,
Bounds our souls tightly

Her Trance

My mind is in a trance
Watching the way that your body slow wine
Feeling my nature beginning to rise
By the way you moving while you dance

The magnetism of the aura you produce
Brings me toward the attraction of wanting
The curves on your body that you're diligently flaunting
Of what God has given you to put to good use.

The temperature is getting hot
But I'm doing what I can to keep my cool
Trying to stay on beat and not look like a fool
And the way that we're touching is really hitting the spot

The way that you bring me in
The way you whispering in my ear
Saying that you loved dancing with me here
And that this feeling should never end.

You begin to move my hands down your side
Until it reaches the stall of your back
Grasping your firm backside like a bear trap
Puts a smile on my face that I can not hide

Your hands are gently stroking my head
You begin to put your lips on my neck
A tingle comes over me that I didn't expect
You've got to let me make you mine I plead

"Sorry". She says." I'm not that easy"
And then she disappears without a trace

Trapped between a rock and a hard place
Of confusion and anger that steamed me.

I lost a Goddess of beauty and dance
That captured my interest and my mind.
I'm sure that we will meet again in due time
Because she will one again traps me within her trance

Behind Closed Doors

When we are behind closed doors,

That's when you see the other side of me,

The side that'll fulfill every pleasure,

Till you reach passion & ecstasy.

I'd kiss your neck & begin to peel off your clothes,

To see what lies beneath,

And when it's only you in your panties,

I'd slowly slide them off with my teeth.

Then I'd open a jar of sweet honey,

To spread over you to lick it off with my tongue,

The fun really hasn't begun just yet,

And yet, your body's already sprung.

I'd move then to your mountains of pleasure,

Moving my lips around down and all over so slow,

Then make my way to your secret garden,

When I'm approaching your valley low.

Licking all around your gates of paradise,

Till you decide to let me in,

And when this snake makes its way through the garden,

That's when the real fun begins.

So when you seem to feel uneasy,

Or everything seems to be a bore,

Be sure to come to this place know one knows,

A place that's behind closed doors.

Love Session

I know this is crazy,
The way that I'm coming at you,
I just can't wait to do,
These things that I love to do,

This is more than just words,
Because this time, I'm going to express,
The love that I have for you
As I begin to caress.

Your neck, your back, your body as a whole,
As you shiver from the softness of my touch,
And when I begin to start to kiss you down low,
I softly whisper to you to hush.

By the shaking in your legs and the noises you're making,
I know that it's about to get loud,
So, I'll change strategy and start at your neck,
But know that I will make myself back down.

Licking between your breast and as I kiss on your chest,
I stop to look you deep within your eyes,
To tell you that I love you and you say it back to me,
Then that is when I push my love inside.

You wanting me to take it slow,
And I obey your every command,
Taking my time to please your body
And then that's when you demand.

To get on top and show me your skill
Of how you love to wine
Man, this feeling you give feels like heaven
And I'm glad you made this feeling mine.

And when we both have reached our peak
Our love session has came to an end
Ant that is when we smile at each other
Cause this session is about to happen again.

Pleasurable

Don't think of me as a freak or pervert,
But there are a million things that I want to do,
To make your body tingle all over,
And make all over your fantasies come true.

I can caress and soothe not only your body,
But also your soul as well,
The passionate love we make is a secret between our lives
Because it's something we'll never speak of or tell

The infatuation that we share between one another,
Along with its sensuality makes it speak louder than words,
The embrace of being as one flows throughout our bodies
Praying that this feeling is not disturbed

Between back rubs, bubble baths, to rose petals in the bed,
Along with strawberries and honey on the side,
Tasting your body is only the beginning,
Of what I've have in mind.

A pleasurable experience that this will be,
A memory you will not want to forget.
A moment of clarity in what love making should be,
A climatic moment you would never expect.

Keep this vision of bliss in your mind
It's all and only for you
Now that I've gave you the warning baby.
It's time I make it do what it do.

The Perfect Storm

You hear that baby.
It's our song.
Well, it's not really a song,
But the rhythm that it plays against the window pane
Leaves our hearts restless.
The lights are off inside of the house
And the only time there's a gleam is when there's lightning.
But this sensation we feel isn't because of that,
It's because of the raindrops.
The raindrops is what draws us closer to each other.
The way it hits the hard surface of something starts a vibration
That hypnotize our mind and takes us to that place.
The place in which there's only me and you
And the quiet storm that's around to mesmerize our mind
And stimulate our sexual tension.
Putting us face to face.
Skin to skin, cheek to cheek.
Making us become one spirit
The way the rain comes down on Earth
Is the way my love comes down on you.
Gentle,cool,in abundance, and able to make your soul
And body wet with ecstasy and delight.
Embracing the feeling of how it feels
To feel this shower of pleasure
Makes me want to be caught in the storm
Of a shower that doesn't need to stop.
No overhead protection should be needed for this.
But as long as it's not a drizzle, then the storm will always be a perfect
one
So tell me baby,
Are you ready to embrace the perfect storm?

Morning Bliss

It warms my heart when I think of this feeling,
It's the only thing I long for when my heart needs healing,

When I have this within my grasp, my soul starts soaring,
It's something that you give me when we wake up in the morning,

I'm not talking about a breakfast in bed,
But a constant thought that runs through my head.

The thought of when we make love,
Feels like something only sent from above.

I feel like I'm in heaven when we become one soul
And if this was a novel, it would be the greatest story ever told.

The way your body stays pressed up against mine,
Makes everything stop at that moment in time.

I cherish your love, your touch, your kiss,
These things that you give me an eternal bliss,

You are my addiction and I don't know what to say,
Cause I find myself wanting you every second of the day

It's like a spell that's been put on my heart
That could easily make me weak if we were to be apart

The passion that runs through our blood which is seen through our eyes
Is more than enough to let me know that this is not a surprise

 That the love is there and it will not be taken away,
And that our love is here to stay.

And hopefully we can keep this thing going,
But let's end it right here and see what happens the next morning

In Control

How can you smile,
When you do these things to me,
To make me reach the point of lust
That's beyond where I need to be.

Strutting around with your red laced panties on,
And some heels on to match
Laying me on the bed with your gentle touch
While you go through with the plan you're about to hatch.

Candles keep the room well lit,
While our favorite song plays in the wind,
You start to dance in front of me place my hands on your hips,
Which lets me know the fun is about to begin.

You kiss me on my neck and chest,
And tell me to not to move,
You begin to climb up on top of me
And start to ride me very smooth.

The speed is just right for this feeling,
I feel like I'm experiencing joy
There's nothing fake about this pleasure you're giving me
This right here is the Real McCoy.

You're having me reach for things to hold
When there is nothing around
I'm trying so hard to keep it calm
But you drive me while with that sexy sound

The moan that comes from you
Makes the passion even more exciting
That I have to put a pillow over my face

And so that I don't scream, I start biting.

Tonight is your night baby
The night that you take hold of my soul.
For you are the one that's calling all the shots,
You are the one that is in control.

Craving

Craving the smell of a good woman to be by my side
Craving the touch that only she can make me feel inside

Craving to be complete when she feels the hole left by another
Craving for her to follow me on a journey that we can both discover.

A journey in which love have no bounds.
Craving for stamina to last with her round for round.

Don't take that as a hint implying to sex
Take that as appreciating the abundance of love she injects

Inside of my bloodstream which courses through my veins
Leaving thoughts of pure bliss swimming through my brain

Craving for her to say my name
When the love becomes passionate and it drives us both insane

Craving the nights when our to bodies merge
With a feeling so strong as if it was a powerful surge

Of energy that goes from one point to the next
Craving to not know what will happen next.

Because I love the way she keeps me on my feet
Like music that you don't want to skip a beat

Her love is my shelter, my fortress, my safe haven
The reason I'm satisfied with her love. The reason I'm craving

Negative & Plus

You make me sick,
But when you're around me, I always feel better
You make me sad when you leave,
But I know that if God's willing, we'll be back together

You make me so damn angry,
But more than that, you make me smile
Sometimes it seems that love has dried up,
But you reinsure that it continually flows like the Nile,

At times I wish you wasn't in my life
But without you, I wouldn't know life at all
I feel like sometimes I'm in a room with no doors,
But you're there to break down those walls.

I know that this sounds confusing
But what now I understand is that with us,
That if I try to think of a negative thing,
There's always a stronger plus.

And when I seem to think I know it all,
You're the one who knows more
And I would have to be a damn fool
If I ever gave up and let you walk out the door

So take heed to what I'm saying
And never try to give up on us.
Cause like I said before, that with every negative
There will always be a greater plus.

S.T.D

Loving to bring pain,
When you go unprotected,
So, practice safe sex

A Hidden Agenda

This agenda of yours was so cleaver

I mean, I wish I could've seen this before all this came to be.

You were my best friend since we were in grade school.

And even after, we became like one.

So, why the deception,

Why couldn't you come to me like a man.

Why would you make this decision that has affected us both.

Now turn around and look at her. Look how she lays in bed.

Cherishing every moment that she spends with you.

But your hidden agenda has gotten the best of you.

So, when are you going to tell her?

When are you going to tell the love of your life that this love isn't real?

That it was something to past up the time of the real agenda at hand

Let's face it, you're not really a womanizer if its not a woman you're cheating

On her with. Yea, now you realize the truth about you.

You've realized what you need to do.

Trust me, it'll only hurt more if you keep it to yourself.

But enough of talking to me.

Quit looking in the mirror and take care of your business.

I Must Not Be There

I should have known from day one
That I would do something to mess this up
Not paying you any attention and being inattentive
Putting my mind upon other stuff

It seems that I've must have been crazy
Or in spirit, wasn't even there
Cause now you're no longer here
And I can't find you anywhere

I'm so sorry for not listening to you
And showing no interest to even bother
But you not being here with me
Makes me not want to see tomorrow

But I made this stupid choice
Praying that I can fix it and it not stay the same
Just know that I'm pouring my heart out in this apology
For treating you're love like a game

But maybe it's best for you at this time to stay away
Cause it's better for you to not be here
Better for you to keep your distance
And for me to get my head clear.

I hope that in time
That you'll come back so I can show you that I care
At this moment though, I would just be a shadow to you.
Because I know that in my mind, I would not be there

Forget Everything

Forget about me ever saying that I care,
Since I'm the only one in this relationship that do,
Forget about us ever being a couple,
Since my love has never meant anything to you.

Forget about the love we'd once made,
Cause now I know that there was never any love there,
Forget about the promises that we both made to each other,
You should bury them and it doesn't even matter where.

Forget about us ever starting a family,
Cause if we had, we would have been living a lie,
Forget about ever wanting you ever wanting to be my wife,
Cause the pain you left within me is enough for me to just die.

Forget about any future for us,
Better yet, just forget about our past,
Forget about trying to work things out now,
Since you were the one who chose not to make it last.

Forget the memories of what used to be us,
And just throw it out the door along with everything else,
Forget about all the nice things I've done for you,
Since you getting treated like crap now that you're with
Someone else.

Now that you understand after being treated like nothing,
The love and passion for you that I wanted to bring,
It's too late because now you don't exist to me,
Cause I've forgotten about everything.

It Is What It Is.

It is what it is when u cant stand still,
It is what it is when u cant pay that late bill,
It is what it is when u grow into love,
It is what it is when u break up wit that scrub,
It is what it is when u wake up glad,
It is what it is when u go to bed mad,
It is what it is when u cherish something close,
It is what it is when u lose the things that meant the most,
It is what it is when drama starts off small,
It is what it is when the drama affects us all,
It is what it is when war breaks out,
It is what it is when out of anger, you'll shout,
It is what it is when u want to be alone,
It is what it is when u feel there's no right without wrong,
It is what it is when I may have just rambled about nothing,
But, it is what it is when u think that this might have meant
something.

By Myself

What's the purpose to being in love
When it seems that your destined to be by yourself
To put some much time into love,
To have it bottled and put on a shelf.

I don't know where to begin this thought,
Cause in reality, it's nothing new,
To give an effort to open my heart,
And find out that love isn't true.

I offered to be there for you,
And help you through the good and the bad,
Now to see that proposal has been shoved away,
I wish that I never had.

Ask to become a part of your life,
Just to keep repeating this same cycle,
At times, I wish that it wasn't love,
And in turn, I wished I just liked you.

So that way when we say that it's over,
I wouldn't feel so upset.
Cause this empty feeling is what I dread the most,
Cause it's a feeling that's hard to forget.

But I do hope that you can find your peace,
And that there's a chance that you will come back to me,
But for now, I'll remain this soulless shell,
Cause for now, by myself is what I'll be.

The Other One

I'm in love with you,
But you belong to someone,
With me on the side

Phone Check

It's hard to believe this silliness,
of what is about to come about,
Trying my best to control my anger,
Trying my best not to shout.

I should've caught on at the jump,
when you'd leave every time you would get a call,
leaving the room and closing the door behind you,
to make sure no one hears you at all.

All the phone calls coming in late at night,
and all the text messages that you'd get,
All the mumbling under your breath,
And all the voicemails you'd always check.

I shouldn't even start to trip,
Because you're my girl and I trust you,
And I know not to fall for love fast,
Plus you know I'm not trying to hurt you.

But here is where you made your mistake,
And believe me that it's an act of God,
Cause you left your cell phone at my house,
And for some reason, I felt kind of odd.

One voice says check the phone,
the other says not to disrespect,
but curiosity has gotten the best of me,
and I had started to go check out her texts.

And there it was clear as day,
What I was hoping that I didn't find,
Now I'm sitting here contemplating

Now's not the time to lose my mind.

Now in comes you, smiling at me,
Asking me how was my day,
I said that it couldn't be better,
And I'd begin to walk away.

But to her surprised, I'd came back
With all her stuff in my hand,
Attempting not to raise my voice,
I told her to go and crawl to her man.

She's begging and pleading of what she did wrong
And I'd showed her dead to her face,
A message from him saying thanks for the loving sweetie,
And her replying that she loved the way he taste.

I hate that I got misled,
Mistreated, misused, and battered like a work glove
You could've spared me the drama,
By not giving me only have of your love

But now it's over, get gone, get out
Plus here's a lesson you should never forget,
Don't give the appearance of you sneaking around,
Or you may be next to fall victim to a phone check.

What Did I Do?

Please tell me, what I did,
To turn you away from this love,
I thought that you were the one,
That heaven had sent me from above,

But now, I find myself putting behind the foolishness,
Of all of the things that you've put me through,
To believe, that I would have gave my life,
For something that I believed was so true.

A kiss from you that seemed sweeter than honey,
Came in turn to be poison to my soul,
I thought that you would never betray my trust,
Cause in my mind, you was what had made me whole.

The universe revolved around only you and me,
And you were the pieces of the puzzle to my love,
I believed that you cared and really had feelings for me
But, like a bully to a kid, your true intentions had begun to shove.

Shove me away. But now you're gone and I stand alone,
With no one to comfort and hold,
No one or nothing to share affection or care for,
Because of the way you've left me. Bitter and cold.

A former shell of a man that once was,
Now nothing more than life past due,
Left standing here with only one question,
What did I do?

Consequence

I can't go through this pain anymore,
Knowing that something will soon end
I wish that we could turn back time
And start our life off as just friends.

Without even thinking of the consequence,
We jumped straight into love,
An at the time, everything was feeling complete
As if it was a blessing sent from above.

Countless hours & endless days
Which make up an infinite time of passion and pleasure
Always wanting you to be in my life
And part of my future endeavors

But who could've seen this coming
Who could have predicted this incident to happen
Blind to the fact that it was predictable
To the point that I'm just sitting here laughing.

The phone call was enough to sense something amidst
Something that would prove terribly wrong
But I didn't pay attention to it.
Because I always tell myself to remain strong.

So now we're sitting together face to face.
Waiting to hear what you have to say
Thinking to myself that what I'm about to hear
Is not important enough to mess up my day.

But, obviously, I was wrong this time
And the joke is on me
Cause you've just told me that your 3 months pregnant
And there's only one person to whom the father could be.

Now, that would make this a happy ending to some
And that should be a better part of my life.
But, it's not because I'm not ready to have a child with this girl
Especially now, cause I have to figure how to get this past my wife.

Hard To Let Go

This is not how I want to feel
It's hard to believe that this concept is real
I hate that I'm living through this painful ordeal
Because it's hard to let go

The love we shared I thought would never end
You weren't just my girl, you were my best friend
Now I wish that I'd never known you back then
Because now, it's hard to let go

And even when you felt sad & alone
You knew that you were always welcome into my home
But this lingering emotion of pain I have makes this so wrong
All because it's hard to let go

I used to feel on top of the world
Cause life for me went to the depths to find you like a pearl
Now it sickens me to see you to the point that I may hurl
Just because it's hard to let go

I even said that I would be a friend to you
To let you know that this love was true
And now I don't even get a call from you
Yet, it's still hard for me to let go

Maybe it's within all of this despair
That I feel that there is something still there
But in turn, you may not really even care
If it's hard for me to let go.

So now, you've left me no choice for life
I have to escape this moment of darkness without light
Now the pain will be over since I've slit my wrist with this knife
Now, I can finally let go

Prison

Never seeing light,
Four walls closing in so close,
Trapped inside my cell.

Five Minutes

Five minutes left to live.
I think of all the things I wished I've could've changed in my life
So many things that could've went my way if I chose that route
But it still won't change the fact that this life of mine is almost over.

Four minutes left to live.
My son and girlfriend come to the jail cell.
I tell them how much I'm going to miss them and cherish this moment
And that nothing will ever take this moment in time away from me.

Three minutes left to live.
My food has come to me and this meal looks exquisite
Every bite is juicy and tasty as if there's life in this meal
But why think about life when mine is about to end soon?

Two minutes left to go.
And the meal was good for the little I ate
But now my mind is focused on what's at hand
On what is about to take place

One minute left.
I hear the footsteps drawing closer, the echoes vibrating on the wall
A pastor comes to read me my last prayer & an officer comes right after
It's time he says. It's time

The walked seemed so long,
The hall seemed so cold and dark
And there it is, the chair
The one thing that will take my last breath away

They strap me in the chair and walk away
I'm staring at people in a sealed room away from me
Then that when they drop the question

Any last words???

That's when I panic
That's when I say to not pull the lever
That's there is something they should know
But know one cares and the lever drops.

I black out but open my eyes.....................
That's when I realize I'm back in the courtroom.
None of what I described has just happened
But the fact that it may occur rest on one thing and one thing alone.

Do I take the fall for my best friend and lose it all cause
Of a 15 year friendship or Lose my best friend for
Destroying his life on a robbery we both committed that went wrong.
What to do???????

Space

The reason for this change is absurd,
Sitting here finding a reason of not understanding
The fact that you want your
Space.
Your time to supposedly collect your thoughts and decide
If what we have is something real
Or a figment of both our imaginations that we let
Run wild and untamed like a forest fire.
So, you leave me here, alone
Soulless, uneasy, and hurt
Because it's not like I did you wrong.
If you were having second thoughts of having a committed
relationship
You should've put it on blast like a public service announcement
Instead of letting it get as far as it has gone
Cause while you're finding yourself after years of building what I
thought was love
You've put me in an area where I'm by myself and the only one who's
standing here looking like an ass.
And yet, as alone as I am, I feel like I'm in my self-established
Space.
Thinking of the reflections of happiness and joy that was once in my
life
But just in a split second, dwindled away like the last little bit of
wicker
Left on the end of a burning candle.
So, what's to say of what is to happen now?
All we can do in this time and age is continued to go on.
Try our hardest not to dwell on the past and make what we have left
of a
Future something that we can live and look forward to.
But the question is.............
If your soul searching takes an eternity

And you then find out that what you had since the beginning
Is what the right thing was really for you to begin with?
What makes you think I will accept you back in my life?
When what you wanted in the beginning was
Space

What Will It Take....

What will it take for you
To see that this is a mistake
A path you shouldn't walk on
A road that you shouldn't take

At a time, you used to love
And care for those around,
But the way you've been lately
Only makes me want to frown

Cause It's sad to see the change in you
Because of the a past sin in which you chose
And now that you're reaping the consequence
The time around those you know have froze.

Cause now they see what you see
And now they're faced with your curse
But now knowing your family knows
Is what's hurting you the worse

So, what will it take my friend,
To stop you from spreading this thing
Cause you're killing the world as we know it
And what joy does this bring?

Because it takes a man to live his life
And what pains that comes with it to bare
But it disgusts me that you're killing through sex
And you don't even care.......

It (A Woman's Story)

I wish I would've never gave it away
It would have been 4 years old today

It could've been something unique & great
It would've been something to start a clean slate

It may have been something to change my ways
It could've been something to brighten my darkest days

I know the world would've loved it in time
And I know back then, I would trade its life for mine

It maybe would have put a smile on my face
Cause Lord knows it's hard to do in this darkened place

It was supposed to be what I'd always wanted
But I wasn't ready for it and now I feel haunted

The outcome of it all was devastating
Before it happened, I found myself hesitating

But we agreed it had to be done
And this decision we made would be an everlasting one

I didn't know if this was wrong or right
And I didn't know what toll it would take on my life

After 4 years of that dreadful decision
Pieces of my life has went through division

Dividing itself away till there's nothing left
I now know that all this time, I was thinking of myself

Considering all that I'd took into absorption
Was the only reason I had gotten that abortion

So every now & then, I cry
Thinking of what its name would've been......Skye

That would've been her name if I let her live
But I chose to kill her/it before I could let life ever begin

Beginnings

The dark clouds began to fade
And the sun begins to shine
Now one again, I pick up the pieces
Of a life once known as mine

I can't let all my pain & sorrow
Be reasons to bring me more down
Cause it seemed like I was lost
But now, I feel like I'm found

The rain that seemed that would never end
Has evaporated off of my mind
To leave nothing but a clear conscious
That came over due time

Even though I've seemed to have lost
So much of my soul & time
Wasteful minutes for something empty
That made me almost lose my mind

But now I am whole again
And I start days a new
No longer a boy but now a man
To live all my days true.

They say that every beginning,
Should always have an end,
I have been through my one beginning.
And I'm going to do my best not to let it end again

LeJuane Bowens was born on July 30,1981 in Detroit, Michigan and moved to Lima, Ohio in 1986 where he went to school and later graduated Lima Senior High in June of 2000. Thinking that he didn't have a chance to get in college, he joined the U.S. Army in August of the same year. Throughout the six years of being in the service, and being deployed to Iraq on two different occasions, he started to put his thoughts on paper. Once starting out as only doing poems of love and lonliness, he started to understand that there is more than life than just two emotions and begin to write about almost everything he felt covered the very aspect of life itself in his eyes.

But it was in the year of 2005 when a friend and fellow poet/writer Keith A. Anderson asked him to take his writing more seriously and try to show the world what he has to say. After deciding to take the advice,LeJuane put a few of his poems on the internet via poetry sites and the feedback that came back from the people that read each one was more than enough to let him know that this may be his calling.

Through poetry, he feels that he can pull people into his world by branching out to them by explaining what he feels are pieces of human nature and will that put together what we all call life. The only thing he wants to achieve is the same thing that everyone wants when they have something on their mind. And that is to only be heard.

So Many Things to Say. A collection of poems covering many things from the aspects of life.Love, lust, adultery, betrayal, war, crime, religion, and rediscovery. You may not want to say what goes on with life, but this collection may be the one thing that will make you open your eyes to what's around and suggest that you reevaluate yourself because when there are so many things to say in this world, it's meant for one thing and one thing only. And that is to be spoken upon.

www.ingramcontent.com/pod-product-compliance
Lightning Source LLC
Chambersburg PA
CBHW031304280526
45784CB00004B/1977